Froggie
Woz Here

Froggie
Woz Here

Iris Howden

Published in association with
The Basic Skills Agency

Hodder & Stoughton
A MEMBER OF THE HODDER HEADLINE GROUP

Orders: please contact Bookpoint Ltd, 39 Milton Park, Abingdon, Oxon
OX14 4TD. Telephone: (44) 01235 400414, Fax: (44) 01235 400454.
Lines are open from 9.00-6.00, Monday to Saturday, with a 24 hour message
answering service. Email address: orders@bookpoint.co.uk

British Library Cataloguing in Publication Data
A catalogue record for this title is available from The British Library

ISBN 0 340 697563

First published 1997
Impression number   10 9 8 7 6 5 4
Year   2005 2004 2003 2002 2001 2000 1999

Typeset by Fakenham Photosetting Ltd, Fakenham, Norfolk.
Printed in Great Britain for Hodder & Stoughton Educational,
a division of Hodder Headline Plc, 338 Euston Road, London NW1 3BH
by Athenæum Press Ltd, Gateshead, Tyne & Wear.

Froggie Woz Here

Contents

1

Grave Digger

Alex was out of work.

He went down to the Job Centre.

'Are you fit?' a man at a desk asked Alex.

'Do you like working outside?

Here's a job as a grave digger.

The money's not bad.

You could start on Monday.'

1

Grave Digger required
Monkton Cemetery
42 hours per week
Good pay

Alex made up his mind. He would take it.

Any job was better than nothing.

He needed the money.

Alex went down to the cemetery.

It was a big place.

Alex asked to see Len.

Len was the head man.

Len was busy.

'I look after this part,' he told Alex.

'You'll have to do all the digging.

I find it's too much for me now.'

He showed Alex the tools.

They sat down. Len told him about the job.

'See you Monday', he said.

'Bright and early.'

2

Trouble

Alex soon got used to the work.

Len showed him what to do.

Then he left him to it.

Alex didn't mind working on his own.

It was quiet, until 4 o'clock.

Then the boys came out of school.

That's when the trouble started.

Some lads took a short cut home.

They ran over the graves.

They kicked over flower vases.

They dropped litter on the neat graves.

One boy had a can of spray paint.

The paint was red.

He left a message on the headstones.

It was always the same –

FROGGIE WOZ HERE.

'Little devil', Len said.

'He can't even spell. Wait till I catch him.'

But he never did.

Froggie was too fast for him.

Froggie was a real pest.

The other lads went off home.

But Froggie stayed behind.

He hid among the gravestones.

Alex would be digging.

A stone would hit him on the neck.

Then one would hit the spade.

Alex looked up.

But there was no-one there.

Sometimes he thought he saw something.

It looked like a boy running.

Alex would hear a vase smash.

He heard someone running off.

Later he would find the message –

FROGGIE WOZ HERE.

3

Alex Strikes Back

'I'll teach him a lesson', Alex thought.

He got an old sheet.

'I'll hide in an open grave,' Alex thought.

'I'll put the sheet over my head.

I'll wait for him and jump out.

He'll have the fright of his life.

He won't pester me again.'

Alex hid just before 4 o'clock.

He left his spade in the ground.

Froggie would find it.

He could never leave things alone.

He touched everything.

Alex waited quietly.

He could hear Froggie coming.

He lay very still.

He felt some soil fall on him.

The lad was kicking it about.

Alex jumped up in his sheet.

'Whoo, whoo, whoo,' he went.

But Froggie didn't turn and run.

He stood there and laughed.

He laughed and laughed.

Froggie pointed at Alex.

'Some ghost, mister!' he said.

'You're mad. Do you know that?'

He tapped his head as he said this.

Suddenly he grabbed the ends of the sheet.

He pulled them round Alex's back.

'Ever been tied in knots?'

he asked in a nasty voice.

Alex fought to get free.

He felt his feet slipping.

Soon Froggie began to slip too.

They both fell into the grave.

Alex made a grab for the spade.

The spade flew out of his hand.

It fell and hit Froggie on the head.

Alex felt the boy go limp.

He pulled off the sheet.

Froggie lay still. His face was pale.

He looked like a small child.

'Oh no, he's out cold!' Alex thought.

'He needs a doctor.'

Alex went to lift him.

He put his hand under Froggie's head.

He saw a pool of blood.

It ran over his fingers.

His shoes had a red stain.

Alex knew that Froggie was dead.

14

4

Hiding

Alex looked around.

The cemetery was empty.

There was no-one there.

Alex began to panic.

He picked up the spade.

And began to dig a hole.

He dug deeper and deeper.

Then he put Froggie at the bottom.

He pulled the sheet over his face.

He covered his body with soil.

Alex worked very fast.

He was shaking all over.

He felt sick.

When Len came by it looked neat.

The grave looked just as it should.

Ready for the funeral next day.

'Come on', Len said. 'Time to go home.

You're very pale. Do you feel OK?

Maybe you've been working too hard.'

Len picked up Alex's tools.

Alex was still shaking.

He dashed out of the cemetery gates.

On TV the next day a man said,

'Police are looking for a missing boy.

He is Martin Frogmore, aged 13.

He has been missing since yesterday.

He was last seen leaving school.

The police want to hear from anyone

who saw Martin after 4 pm yesterday.'

Alex turned the TV off.

He felt sick and cold.

The name Martin Frogmore

kept going through his head.

He closed his eyes and said –

'It was just an accident.

I didn't mean to harm him.

I just wanted to teach him a lesson.'

The TV screen shows: MISSING SCHOOLBOY

Alex waited for the police to come.

But they never came.

No-one else had been in the cemetery.

No-one had seen Froggie there.

Then a boy spoke to the police.

He told them about a man.

The man had been hanging around the school.

He had talked to some boys.

Maybe he had talked to Froggie.

The paper took up the story –

HUNT FOR MISSING BOY GOES ON.

The police want to talk to a man.

He was seen outside the school.

He had a blue car.

The police looked and looked.

They talked to lots of people.

Alex saw the TV news each night.

Soon there was nothing about Froggie.

The case was closed.

Alex knew it was OK.

He would get away with it.

He wanted to give himself up.

It had been an accident.

He wanted to tell the police.

But it was too late.

The funeral had taken place.

Another body was on top of Froggie's.

Alex couldn't go to the police now.

It would cause too much trouble.

5

The Last Laugh

Alex went to work as normal.

He did his job as he always did.

The papers had other stories:

A plane crash, a bank raid.

No-one thought about Froggie.

No-one except Alex.

He thought about him every day.

Alex stayed away from Froggie's grave.

He didn't like being near the grave.

It was spooky.

A few weeks went by.

Alex had to work near Froggie's grave.

He did not look at the grave.

He worked quickly.

He looked at his watch.

It was nearly 4 o'clock.

'Ping!' a stone hit his spade.

Another stone hit his neck.

Alex jumped. He spun round.

No-one was there.

Then he saw a dark shape.

It was running between the graves.

Alex heard footsteps.

He turned around quickly.

No-one was there.

Then he heard a crash.

A vase lay broken on a grave.

Alex waited.

He was afraid.

His heart began to pound.

Then he heard a boy's laugh.

He ran towards the sound.

Then he stopped.

On a grave was a message.

It was in red paint. It was still wet.

It looked like blood. It said –

FROGGIE WOZ HERE

Alex turned cold.

He thought –

'Is somebody playing a game?

Or has Froggie come back from the dead?'

He could still hear a boy's laugh.

It was Froggie's laugh.

Alex dropped his spade.

He ran to the cemetery gate.

Len saw him go.

He shouted after him –

'What's the matter?

You look as though you've seen a ghost.'